What They Don't Tell You

About Mourning

Erika Hiwiller

This is dedicated to:

Eric Hiwiller

Ben Davidson

Daniel Davidson

Winifred and Robert Truesdale

Randy and Jack Smith

Susan and Josh Hermann

Ezra Dean

Samson and Stormy

Jinkx

And

Every other ghost

Who brought us

To the place

We're supposed

To be.

They'll tell you
That life goes on.

They'll tell you
Everything will be okay.

They'll tell you
It comes in waves.

They'll tell you
That everything happens for a reason.

They'll tell you
This too shall pass.

They'll tell you
The feeling is temporary

They'll tell you
All about heaven

And while sometimes
These words will ring true,

There is so much more we need
To know about mourning.

They didn't tell me
That I would tear up
Sporadically in public.

They didn't warn me
That emptiness could reach
Places he had never touched.

They didn't help me
When I reached out
And felt nothing.

They didn't show me
The right way to deal
With the constant choking.

They didn't know me
When I passed them
And was ignored.

They didn't hold me
When my grip
On this world had slipped.

So now, I'll tell you
The things no one told me
About mourning.

They don't tell you
That time moves forward.
But you will be stuck
Reliving that day
For months

They don't tell you
How cold it can
Feel in August.
And how even his jackets
Cannot thaw the ice

They don't tell you
His absence
Will make loneliness
Weigh more than
The casket he lies in

They don't tell you
That you have to decide
What kind of flowers to buy
And whose name goes in the paper
And every other decision
That means absolutely
Nothing
To you, but everything
To those who did not wake up
Numb.

They don't tell you
Not everyone will understand
The way each breath
Feels like a betrayal.
And each step
Takes more energy
Than every power plant
Can produce.

They don't tell you
Your bones will feel borrowed
And your skin paper thin
Your tongue will be thick and heavy
Tears will fall down your face
And not feel wet.

They don't tell you
That some people will find
Nothing but jealousy in their hearts
And manifest anger
That even I,
Cannot explain.

There are very
Few things
I feel
Comfortable
Calling myself
An expert in

But loss
And funerals,
Mourning
And recovery

I feel
Qualified
To give
Certified advice.

The day began with a thunderstorm.

We drove through it

road after road blocked by fallen trees

as if the Universe knew

we were not meant to leave.

The weather cleared,

and the call came,

something happened.

He didn't make it.

"Mommy" the little girl said.

"How's grandma going to get to heaven?"

What do you mean? – she answered

"She doesn't know how to drive."

She doesn't need to know how to drive

She'll spread her wings

and fly.

You will know

when the world stops spinning

because everything will continue

exactly the same,

but look completely different.

It will make you think of all the times

you walked around focused on your daily life

unaware of the tragedies beyond.

They wouldn't let me see him

as the police fluttered in and out

and his dog barked

protecting him from being taken away

only stopping

when I held her.

                                       -we probably smelled the same.

He was over six feet tall,

but his body fit in that bag.

No one warned me,

that the arms that held like pillars

my entire life

could look so small.

The bag was white.
The gurney was black.
And that sight
took every ounce of color
from my world.

Some people cry,

Some are still,

Some feel numb,

I screamed my bloody head off.

-reactions to getting the call

You didn't know
the phone was on
speaker.
You didn't know
I was in
the car.
You didn't know
how loud I
could scream.

I'm sorry
if I scared you.

They asked me

if I wanted my own urn

to hold some of his ashes

or a necklace

to carry him

wherever I go.

But I thought,

will I get

the arm bone

or a toe

or an eye.

I didn't want him

separated

piece by piece

so I left him be whole

-A mini urn is $30

I was afraid
of the casket
to reach out
and touch
the pale
lifeless
corpse
and feel
the cold
skin
that had
before
radiated
more heat
than the
sun.

I did not know how
to verbalize my fear
that the funeral
would be as full
as an abandoned house.

So I started
selling tickets
to make sure
he had a full
stadium.

To my surprise, my efforts
were unnecessary.
People showed up in droves.
The seats were as full
as my heart.

-standing room only

I have always had
an irrational fear of mirrors.
I feared for souls getting trapped.
I always wondered
when I looked at my reflection
who was looking back at me.

The funeral home had three
mirrors, uncovered.
I spent the days there,
blocking them,
just in case.

She's fighting demons of the thought,
that she should have saved him.

He attacks everyone,
he should be holding close.

She thinks the mother,
should have gone first.

No matter how much time passes,
Guilt maintains his grip.

His (ex)wife got everything.

-Divorce crazy bitches as soon as possible

Things I had Been Told:

He's in a better place now.

He'll always be with you.

He's happier now.

Let me know if you need anything.

Sorry for your loss.

Everything happens for a reason.

It's not that big of a deal.

Things That Were not Helpful

He's in a better place now.

He'll always be with you.

He's happier now.

Let me know if you need anything.

Sorry for your loss.

Everything happens for a reason.

It's not that big of a deal.

Things I Had Been Told

Part II

He told me all the time how proud he was of you.

I'll make sure you're not alone

He talked about you all the time.

I love you.

He loved you.

Things That Actually Meant Something

He told me all the time how proud he was of you.

I'll make sure you're not alone

He talked about you all the time.

I love you.

He loved you.

The world
will appear quite dull
your water
will taste just
ever so slightly
like trees
the air
will begin
to smell
like
uncooked meat
gentle hugs
might leave
cuts
and every
voice
will be
a siren,
including
yours.

I dreamt of him.

I was in a car.

He was outside of it.

A giant black jaguar emerged

from the shadows.

We got in the car

and drove away

-safe and sound

I wasn't there when I lost my childhood.

-Ezra Dean

His death was a warning
of what was to come.

The image of him
giving **CPR** to my cat,
was the first trauma.

-mourning pets is just as valid

Death refused me,

the luxury of a build-up.

The ones I love,

were there one minute,

and gone the next.

                                        -just once, let me say goodbye

I didn't go back to work
I gave myself ten days to be sad
before going back to school.

                              -He'd rise up and kill me
                                  if I took a year off

I'd go through moments
where I couldn't tell the
difference,
between mourning you,
and being jealous
it wasn't me.

Who died?
Your grandson.
Oh. Which one?
My son.
Who?
Your grandson.
Did he have any kids?
A daughter.
Who died?

-Overheard conversations
-Death and Dementia

How was your summer?
My dad died.
How was yours?

-A natural conversationalist

She uses it as an excuse.

It wasn't that big of a deal.

No one cares.

-Overheard Conversations Part II

This semester has been the most challenging yet.
He says to me,
I read hundreds of pages every night.
He adds.
It's been rough for me too,
I say to him.
My dad died in August.

-A natural conversationalist Part II

Did you know
Mourning has symptoms
That emerge
in different
colors
depending on
the person.

The symptoms can spread
not from person to person
but from your heart
to your head.

My symptoms
were red and blue.
Red for the
constant panic
that everything was on fire,
because it was.

And at the same time
blue for the color
my lips were slowly turning
from how cold
every room was
without you.

Death led me to battle
not only myself,
but everyone who encouraged my drowning.

I would dig my

fingernails

deep, into my flesh

until the skin broke

to bleed

just a tiny bit.

-My outsides needed

to match my insides

His dog died,

one month after him.

They said seizure.

I said heart break.

Now when I envision him

watching over me

I get to see

a six-foot-something man

carrying his very tiny yorkie.

-the image makes me smile

The August storms,
took him,
when they rolled through.

Now thunderstorms,
are his visits,

Leaving raindrop kisses,
and lightning *I love yous.*

August Rain

Today the sky is bleak
It is my favorite,
to know that even the sunshine
takes a break.

People complain when it rains
the inconvenience is offensive.
It interferes with their plans
and ruins their day.

But I like the rain.
I like how my hair gets messed up
and everyone else is disheveled
and no one is expected to look perfect.

I like when it is just a sprinkle
because then it lightly splashes my face
like from the sink in the morning
I am reminded I can breathe.

I like the way it smells.
It soaks deep into the soil
to release an earthy aroma
to keep everything alive.

I like whenever it pours.
It soaks through my clothes,
deep into my skin.
making me reborn again.

My dad used to watch the storms.
He would stand on the porch
and gaze at the purple sky as it crashed
and not be afraid.

It stormed in August.
Wind screamed through the trees
water filled the streets
and my dad stopped breathing.

I knew he was never afraid of storms
because of this I never understood
how other people,
could hate the rain.

It was the rain that took my father
but it was not the thunder,
nor the lightning,
but the storm that brewed inside of him.

Every grey sky
every strike of purple lighting
every fallen wayward tree
makes me think of him.

I love the wind,
the way it can blow through my skin.
I love the thunder,
and how the sound rattles my bones.

I love the lightning
and the sublime feeling I get.
I love the flood
knowing any moment I might drown.

To this day,
I can say that I find comfort in the rain
I know that sometime soon I will face that purple sky
and not be afraid.

In one year,

I saw a stroke,

a heart attack,

an overdose,

and so many

ghosts.

I was named

after two men

two fathers

Brothers

Husbands

who died

and left behind

Daughters

with only ash.

-Eric and Daniel

I spent the rest of summer
in a sweatshirt
constantly sweating
and still feeling cold.
standing in front of the sun
imagining the light
could be swallowed
and warm my insides.

Sometimes I wear his jacket and pretend it's a hug.

The Five Stages of ~~Grief~~ Bullshit

They described grief as an uphill battle,
passing five marked stages
following road signs until
an exhausted mourner
reaches the top of the mountain.

My mother told me
grief is an ocean
and I am a surfer
riding waves
trying to stay afloat.

My experience has met all five stages
but not through road signs
and some, once they
introduced themselves
became a constant companion.

Denial introduced himself
immediately
He crawled into my mind
and acted as a barrier
to fend off the nasty
reality I found before me.

He made sure to
make it so I would not
soak it all in at once.
He still visits every morning
splashing my face with sunshine
before the storm clouds return

Bargaining was a stranger I passed
a fleeting thought I made
sure to offer
the Universe
my life in exchange for his.
But the stranger and I
made eye contact
and went our separate ways

Depression moved into my mind
signed a one-year lease
and became a hermit.

Anger and Denial like to wrestle
while Depression looked on,
quietly sipping tea
watching the show in front of her
until everyone went back to
their own private corners

Anger only visited on occasions
when I remembered
all that was taken.

Acceptance was always around.
A neighbor in a different building,
who heard all the commotion
coming from my mind.
But she would sit outside,
quietly
waiting until I came to greet her
so she could walk me home.

When the cloud lifts
you'll feel lighter,
but slightly uncomfortable.

I spent the next year

terrified

of my phone

every time it would ring.

-Side Effects

I was constantly cold

numb to physical pain

and constantly worrying

that my house was burning down.

-Side Effects II

The perfect mourner
is a ghost.

I had another dream
you weren't there.
it was just me
alone
in an empty room
lying in a hospital bed
I felt nothing
but calmness
as I slowly slit
my own throat
and reached inside
to pull out my
lungs
one at a time,
desperate
for the pain to bring release
but it never came,
paralysis
in my torn body
until I awoke
in a cold sweat
It was that moment I realized
how not okay
I truly was.

The hardest moments
are when
I choke up in public.

Like a doctor
asking if he's still
my emergency contact

Or my school,
asking why every letter mailed
gets returned.

                              -the cardboard box full of ash
                           in my grandmother's spare room
                                   does not have an address

The clichés hit hard first,

knowing you won't walk me down the aisle

or kiss your grandchild's cheek.

You won't read my first book.

Little did I know,

you'd be the topic.

I was born between two souls.

The rigid strength of my mother,

whose backbone can bear the weight

of every burden demanded by the Universe.

And the Spontaneity of my father,

who roamed with the freedom of a bird,

whose wings were just too heavy

to take flight.

none of the ghosts have graves to haunt

-looks like I'm the only option

The matted stuffed cat,

From the hospital giftshop,

The plushie pup,

Won from a carnival game,

The tiny diamond necklace,

Gifted to me twice,

The unfocused pictures,

Taken many years ago,

A tattered hoodie,

From a Christmas long since past

-a list of things worth more than their weight in gold

I'm still mad at myself,
for spilling soup on that jacket..

                                        -I had to wash out the smell

I had one more dream,
where we gathered at my grandparents
and I commented on the
amount of food in the fridge
because someone
hadn't been around to eat it.
and you tapped me on the shoulder
and laughed.
then showed me a chalkboard
with my name
and your parents'
and your sister
with every date
since you died
with a big red check mark
beside every name
under every
single
date.

Thank you for showing me
you're always here

I have his curls
his bushy, untamed eyebrows
the pale, constantly sunburnt skin,
a shared desire for a Hogwarts letter,
and his name.

-Legacy

Eventually,

I forgot about my memory loss.

Remembering details,

was at one point

my strength.

I lost that,

when I lost you.

-grief brain is real

When they called the ambulance

it went one house too far

down to a home they had

been called to time and time again

                                                        -precious time wasted

                                            -I have to forgive them every day

When I say I'm getting bad again

I don't mean

I'm sad

or angry

or full of rage

I mean that I feel absolutely nothing.

                                        -the most dangerous feeling

Losing you was painful,

dealing with them,

was unbearable.

It took me many years, to understand

why those girls singled me out.

Everyone told me it was jealousy,

but it never made sense

what I had that they wanted.

Did they want to share my grief?

Were they envious of the sleepless nights?

Now, years later, I understand.

My life was so full,

even though I was living

as if it was empty.

I curled my lips as I spoke

and yanked my limbs inside my torso.

I pulled out hair one strand at a time

and let my skin dehydrate.

-they made me feel small

It was almost amazing

to watch how quickly

the colors of their hearts

were revealed,

as they ripped them out

and placed them in front of me.

My first public poetry reading
was at a funeral.

I Know You Didn't Know Him

Walking down the street, we don't realize the impact we have

In the building you just passed, without as much as a glance

A Soul is recently lost

Nothing but his Shell remains

That boy, that man, didn't mean anything to you

Understandable

He was just a common person

No

He was much more than that

Every person makes a difference

Every Soul that has ever been created makes an Impact

That man was a Father, a Son, a Brother, an Uncle, a Cousin,

He had a family

To which his life had more influence than he will ever be around to know

He didn't know that though

He felt the same way about himself as you

He didn't know how special each person is.

He was unaware that our lives, they're interconnected

Every single person who has ever spoke, and even those who haven't

They each have a direct effect on the people they come in contact with

I know you didn't know him

I didn't really either

I wish I had

I hate how our backwards judgments drive people to such extremes

But it seems our world is not capable of change

Only Progress

I hope I live to see a world where

Each boy and each girl

Are able to rise above any pain

But nowadays that is not possible, and we are not yet Capable

But I see a Chance for us to Change

I think each of us can use these deaths and this destruction

We can use this negativity to band together and create something
more powerful

Life is not to be wasted or to make people feel like they are not
worthy

We all make a difference to someone

We all mean something

Our Choices, Actions, Words, Thoughts, Prayers, Hopes, Dreams,
Desires

They each make someone else's life worth living

So next time if you're walking down the street

And hear a woman sobbing

Don't think less of her for trying to overcome her pain

He meant something to us

I hope you never have to experience the same

This is dedicated to All the people

Who have ever been that person walking down the street

Unaware of the utter disaster that has just unfolded

I know I have been there, I just am not sure when

I know you didn't know him

I didn't really either

I wish he had given me the chance

Cardinals

started appearing to me

in the dead

of winter.

I knew the exact moment
I started to feel better.
when I imagined
my own death,
and watched the girl
lie in her bed
with her wrists
bleeding out
and thought,
I hope someone finds her in time.

-Different people

On the anniversary
of his death
we all gathered
and released lanterns
in the sky.

One year later,
we were scattered.
And I know the ones
who remembered
and the ones who did not.

We have had enough funerals,

we no longer needed family reunions.

I only wrote

a couple poems

during the first year...

There's a bruise on my leg and

I like it

I like it because when I poke it, it hurts

And it hurts because my outsides

Are beginning to look like my insides

But my insides are torn to pieces and

My insides hurt when you poke it

But you can't see the pain

When people see the bruise they ask if I'm okay

But when I say my dad died

They just look like they can't be bothered

That's because it's okay to be in pain

If it's physical

But the second you show that it's emotional

You're suddenly weird for not being able to handle it

There's a cut on my finger and

I like it

Because when I squeeze it, it bleeds

Just like my heart

But when my heart bleeds you can't see that either

So I just let my chest fill up with blood

And drown

I'm losing weight and people say congratulations

They say congratulations because I am not eating my feelings

But the truth is I'm not eating at all.

I can pull my belt two holes tighter

Which is the reward I got

When I lost my will to live

It's not okay to be depressed but

It's much worse to be depressed and fat

Or so they tell me

Because of this my insides are hollow

The air that fills them is cold

I shake constantly but

If anyone asks I can say that I am just cold

And not be at all lying

When I say I am cold

People offer to get me a jacket

But when I say I numb from the inside out

They tell me to keep that to myself

The skin under my eyes is turning black and blue and

People ask if I'm getting enough sleep

They want a yes or no

But when I say I dream of fire and

Cannot seem to find rest

They tell me to count sheep

But no matter what I still open my eyes

And everything is still on fire

What does the perfect mourner look like?
Does she cry in dignified silence?
As the wailing is reserved for those without control.

Does she graciously accept
every condolence offered
by those pretending to care?

Is she sad for the
perfect amount of time
not too long, but not too short?

Does she never feel anger
at herself for feeling
or at him for leaving?

Does she dress in black
so that others know
she is to be avoided?

It was exactly seventeen months after
when I felt the relief.

-everyone's timeline is different

I realized
all these emotions
were wrapped in
a big blood-soaked bow
named mourning

-its own beast

There is nothing wrong with you.
You are a fighter,
And a survivor.
You will overcome
because of
and in spite of
everything you've been through.

It's not about me.

It's about keeping

the ghosts happy.

When I search my name all I see are obituaries.

My pencil scratching paper stops
my nails from scratching skin.

Things that got me through:

Taylor Swift's Reputation

Friday's spent along the Little Shenango

Harry Potter Marathons

The dreams

Memories

And myself.

There came a point
where I felt like
I could not talk about it.
the time for mourning
was over
as far as so many
were concerned.

-Time moves slower when you're mourning

Sometimes,

hearing your name

sends me back in time.

I learned, if you spend your time fearful,

you end up living through it twice.

-a mantra

We didn't take enough pictures.

-my biggest regret

I spend my life
living my back-up plan
because my real ambition
faces failure
and I cannot
take such risks
when I am
living for
two.

My back up plan is a boa constrictor,
that began to wrap around my ankles,
and tripped me as I walked.
Until it slithered up to my throat,
and slowly choked
the life out of me.

You weren't the only one I told
I wanted to be a writer.

You were the only one
Who didn't make it seem impossible.

Writing makes my body vibrate,
my soul hum,
and my truth feel spoken.

The fear of failure adds weight to my chest,
chalk in my mouth
and spreads falsehoods of joy.

I heard your voice
today
Loud and clear.

Get up.
You said
and I looked
around the room

and I was met
with silence
and white walls
and I knew
it had to be you

Sometimes,
it feels like
we talk more now
that you're gone
than we did
when you were
here.

I've been so much happier
since I started writing again.

My poetry is the cliché metaphor of a phoenix rising

from the ashes.

Only those ashes do not belong to me and I live in

fear of these particles of dust as one day I must

return to that fate.

From tragedy, poets are born.

But we do not enter this life easily.

We fight with razor sharp pens ready for battle.

We spill ink in the wake of trauma.

We cauterize our wounds with the aching stitches

made from notebook paper.

Our tears are boiling water

that cleanse the filth from our souls.

We cry out to others for the sake of some much-availed salvation, but

somehow continue to lose

sight of our goal,

to be remembered.

For a brief time

I lost my faith in the Universe.

All I could count on

was more being taken.

Until I realized,

you would be there

pulling strings.

I try daily
to write about love.
but soon I realized,
writing about their death
was how I showed them
love.

Eventually, there came a point

when I needed

to stop focusing on the

obituaries already written

and start focusing

on living beyond that paragraph.

Two years later,
I get up
and brew coffee
and do yoga
and shower
and journal
and get ready
and go.

Two years ago,
I got up.

-progress

In Lieu of Flowers

Why is it
that death and flowers
go hand in hand?
As if the gift
of wilting petals
will serve as
something other than
a constant reminder
that decay is inevitable.

In lieu of flowers,
send a bouquet of love,
wrapped with a red ribbon
and sealed with a kiss.

I do not remember
a single person
who sent me flowers.
I remember every person
who went out of their way
to shower me with their light.

In lieu of flowers,
send a meal homecooked in hope,
with reminders that it is
not treacherous
to avoid starving.
Allow the feelings
of hope and love
to fill the emptiness.

In lieu of flowers,
send yourself
shrink wrapped in time
devoted to simply being
present in the moment.
Time may not heal wounds
completely,
but it will help
stop the bleeding.

Overall,
please know,
you are not alone.
There is nothing
more human
then trudging through
the darkness
towards the beacon
of light
that awaits you.

Acknowledgements:

There are so many people to thank for making this collection of poetry come together. Thank you to every friend and family member who proofread and gave feedback. Thank you to every person who encouraged this endeavor, without whom I might not have had the courage to publish this collection.

Thank you to Md Mahbub Alam for designing the cover of this book.

Thank you to the people who have come and gone from my life, leaving their mark and allowing me to create this collection.

And many thanks to you, dear reader. Thank you for taking the time to delve into this collection, that truly is my own heart and soul presented before you. I wish you all the love and light this world has to give.

Authors Note:

Thank you for taking the time to read this collection. Now please listen to something happy, meditate, draw yourself a warm bath. Do whatever it is you do in the name of self-care. Delving into this darkness and emerging with your head above water is no easy feat. It is exhausting and you must recharge.

You have just traveled a long journey through the depths of what I am sad to say is the universal human emotion of grief. Please know that the heaviness does eventually lighten and seek help if you are unable to bare the load. Emotional trauma and pain is very real and just as devastating to the body and mind as anything physical.

Follow @spirit.poetry for more content.

Made in the USA
Columbia, SC
26 June 2020